Mount Sumptuous

Aidan Coleman

**Wakefield
Press**

Wakefield Press
16 Rose Street
Mile End
South Australia 5031
www.wakefieldpress.com.au

First published 2020

Cover design by Liz Nicholson, Wakefield Press
Typeset by Michael Deves, Wakefield Press

ISBN 978 1 74305 664 6

A catalogue record for this
book is available from the
National Library of Australia

Wakefield Press thanks
Coriole Vineyards for
continued support

For Beatrice, Louis & Wilfred

Some power that hardly looked like power
Said I'm perfect in an empty room
– *The Wild Kindness*, Silver Jews

Contents

Acknowledgements

The poems in *Mount Sumptuous* were published in the following journals, newspapers, and anthologies: *Australian Book Review, Australian Poetry Journal, Australian Poetry Journal Anthology 2015, 2016 and 2018, Best Australian Poems* 2014 and 2016, *Blackbox Manifold* (UK), *BlazeVOX* (US), *The Carolina Quarterly* (US), *Coolabah – Observatori: Centre d'Estudis Australians* (ESP), *Cordite Poetry Review, Glasgow Review of Books* (UK), *The Hampden-Sydney Review* (US), *Island, Lindenwood Review* (US), *Meanjin, Meniscus Literary Journal, North Dakota Quarterly* (US), *Otoliths, Overland, Poetry Salzburg Review* (Austria), *Right Hand Pointing* (US), *The Stockholm Review of Literature* (Sweden), *States of Poetry: Australian Book Review* (SA) (print and online), *SWAMP, Tincture Journal, Virginia Quarterly Review* (US), *The Weekend Australian*, and *Westerly*.

Some of these poems appeared in the Southlands Poets' Chapbook Series under the title *Cartoon Snow* (Garron Publishing, Adelaide, 2015).

Many thanks to the SA writing community for their camaraderie and support, particularly Ken Bolton, David Cornish, Matt Hooton, Banjo James, Jill Jones and Thom Sullivan. My gratitude also to Tess Coleman, David Moseley, Pei Shu Wu for permission to use the cover image; and to my family – Leana, Beatrice, Louis and Wilfred – for their patience, love and inspiration.

Oracular

Don't ask me the wind whispers,
and when you check
next door, you can't be
heard over road-rage and the dark
pulse of stadia. You forget
your shopping in a lyric
flourish: presidential

hopefuls – shifting
in their blue and red stables –
can't shape late talk to fit
a dreaming-space. Among
a harvest of fanatics, clever heads
on panels won't stop.

Cartoon Snow

When your freezer is cluttered
as a library returns chute
you realise the benefits of

cartoon snow. The sugar
cubes of igloo bricks,
well-storied in their

crisp divisions. The daybreak
of those dazzling acres
you would dress for.

Go when a blue night
is snowing to itself, shushing
the owl-wide forest.

How gently it erases
fox-prints and sleigh-tracks,
the stamp of hoof

and hunter's boot,
the vexatious sharp edges
of our pasts.

Retire once more
to the puffing cottage,
its windows a blazing marmalade.

Inside, the huskies
have quit their howling
to settle for the uncluttered life:

the idea of North.

The End of Weather

There's a way summer stops
short of nudity
like a lo-fi Santa providing own beard.
The loose delight of your task
necessary as twins
coordinating shirts and comedy.
The exhibition match scheduled for rain.
A trainee nuances Auslan
for a cyclone called Greg. Though real,
Greg is late for the election,
can hardly help the damage
he will wreak.

Primary

My first car red as a half-sucked
Jaffa, the crackling bacon
of its radio. The brick of all-meat
towns you dress
to kill on Fridays. The O
of mouths and round
of targets – you recall, in panic-big letters,
the shiny apple from a story

best avoided. *Red is not
my favourite colour* the child screams,
over khaki shorts and wounded knee.
Now the teacher chastens gently
in lowercase green.

Nth Degree

You crowd
          into a taxi and the plates
      fall off. Tight blue
       parents in the suburbs
          of their constancy.
  Pass yourself –

      racing through
catalogues
        of aftershave –
a grappling hook
      wedged in the thigh
          of Mt Sumptuous.

Adventures in Reading

I.

Intentions flash past like jet skis
or a Gopher at speed
when the view is narrowed by excess staff
and pot plants.

2.

Locked as a banana
to the very young
and now a peel to slip on
for undercover work at a tropical fruit-themed party.

3.

As irrelevant glitter sticks
in your throat, you gesture toward an inner nudity –
dressing hurriedly to uphold
a sense.

4.

Muzak floods the café
drowning most
but your book a kickboard with which to float
until they switch on breakfast.

Holiday Skies

Between the poems to help
and the news
that isn't, this day

humming like unopened mail.
When you check
the park is on,

the lake too:
coots, down and up,
like pump-cars,

the chipper plans
of ducks on shortwave;
not a care in the sky,

and the old swing
creaking like a seagull.
Late and wary parents balance

keep-cups and disposables,
kids run rings
around the playground's

bright entanglement.
Squadron on squadron
of Rotarians bussed in,

every possible dog,
and geese, as always,
pushing their luck

beside the camouflage
of the pink
and sonorous ice cream truck.

Immortal Diamond

The do-it-yourself piano isn't
kicked to matchwood, and you take this
for affirmation. When we work out
how to switch off Bob Dylan,

your plangent homemades will go
unaccompanied, no longer sought
like an injury lost in the mists

of Hansard. Friends suggest topics
you won't be using, and this
is more like an archive sneeze
than what yesteryear's beard in physics

said it could be. Quite unlike
the night beyond, snowing
sheet after perfect sheet of stars.

Band|Aid

Animals attack whichever celebrity,
everything else

can be summed up as tennis.
Statues yanked out

and the squares fill
with custard. Day's equation

adjusts incrementally
for agile pushers, precarious

trucks. Darks and neons
plucked from our mouths

before we can ask.
What of those shades of menace

we lost, simply a matter of costume?
Your plane dropped eggs

on hapless villains,
who – accordingly chastened –

went home.

Room Temperature

Like a knighthood for cold storage,
most careers lounge in the shade
of their usefulness. At least

the proud, bright sail
of a TED Talk keeps fitting us
to our own good. The relief

it is to see the nearest collector
deep in text. Calamities light
with sudden bouquets. There can

never be too many thumbs,
too few sets of words
to get around or hang a doubt on.

Unready

A cry swerves into sleep.
              You wake
a parent.

Secondary

Angling over
star-fields, the pitches lit like billiard tables.
Those lengths you were shouted up
and back, lungs scoured
by Brillo air. The lazier concord
of close mown grass and low hanging fruit
of the short boundary. A tang
of primitive electronics: the circuit board's
braille labyrinth, the slab type
of Amstrad.
This callow path you cannot take
curves around and through the way a perfect river
might. You find a little gate unlatched
and the light tangles, as you step
into the ferment, into the heady reek of itch.

AI

Meanwhile
we're waiting to buy coffee
with hardly a glitch or risk

to staying in bed.
For now, our texts are mis-
corrected; this film,

as Skynet, too self-aware.
At least the poem,
like retro-gaming,

is safe as submarines
from tanks,
so even an army

of volunteers can't cajole
the keynote speaker
to doctor wounds

at short notice.
A West Texas accent
opens doors

in West Texas;
your work remains
remote, a controlled fortress.

Logos, as in Brands

I.

Hips on stereo in all their veracity:
could poetry be that inflatable
logo? Take the juiceless fruits
of day labour and a white

goods salesman's leaden chicanery.
Among exhortations on the aisle
untaken, a single phrase flashes
its beautiful teeth.

2.

Flammable as *Best & Less*
and more difficult to return
your feelings. The gauge

narrowing to universals.
Horizons clutter with drones
bumping into each other.

3.

You catch yourself in the cast
of *The Thinker*, bored

on the cover of *Why?*
Better aboard a yacht charting

unaudited waters. Beauty
is fleeting but dumb

forever, coached Judge Judy,
but still the tissues show

the stupid faces of princesses.
For bad behaviour that year

I got one encyclopaedia.
I think it was F or U.

Diagram & Leaf

If
at the wrong hour
the street turns out its pockets
kings or cowards will be
named. There's ever
an argument to talk your way
down from, playing late on the radio.
A forgetful city is always becoming,
making our arrival.
Leaky packages, tricks
on paper, long afternoons
by sparkling water –
the theorem behind obsidian
and mirror.

Motivational

Fitness: fact, fiction
or fantasy? – among things
meant. Parachutes

open like fuchsias,
picnic hampers
of kittens float quietly

down, as peaks
push through
resplendent mists.

Your sense
falls upward
like helium or blinds,

now it's precisely
subtitled, you realise –
while the first tentative

steps emerge
to be recorded
as a baby.

Consider the aspirin
in its exuberance
that picks itself up

and turns itself over
to become
no other than

water and air.
Like effusive, ever-
digressive chatter –

you could.

Courtier

Say you're a goldfish in the late '80s
with no more room to move
than a Blue Light Disco.
The torture
of yard and given names
from soaps selling dads at the Weber.
Where mirror balls hang like the planets,
tongues peel each other
from rumour.
As back-masking recedes
into a smooth future,
you push through the stuttering fray,
towards your best friend's older brother,
who knows the DJ, and ask him how to get there.

Regent & Seal

In the wreckage of his waking,
the infant slumbers.

Moderate

The chorus falls between
the words I read

to ignore the scenery,
like the prayer

for speed and safety
you forget

to hang up from.
Whichever dawn or sale

is tweeted, a line
will be drawn

to cross or hold.
Our century

(by which I mean here)
will brook no

neck-verse.
Any way you monster it

my dentist is friendly
and careful.

To the only begetter

For WH

Like rope and pulley work to hold up pink
and stodgy cherubs. Like the apple of my
iPhone, faint of charge. Like the superfluity
of bikers' arms or the big and little words
of lovers' cells. Like the stylised tantrum
of youth rejecting the tutelage you feigned.
Like shy graffiti or the bling of cases. Like
the cashing trees. Like toddlers hovering
at the margins, where dragons used to be,
or a high-speed ransack of outdoors.
Like sudden mushrooms blooming pages
between or the screwdriver of your pocket
knife taken to canvases. Like your skywriting
jet gunned down mid-cliché. These trifles.

Contingencies

Your
sentiment

tangles
with data

where
analysts

covering
bases

uncover
fresh

affronts
a well

rounded
baby

wakes
assuming

parents

The Shorter Shakespeare

1.

what might you carry into boardroom into battle

2.

halls of dead and prose sleepwalkers

3.

a knife fight before heavy mortars

4.

had one word fallen different

5.

your ships a pop-up book

6.

it's not easy being king

7.

melting down caskets

8.

a trumpet within

9.

loaned ears

10.

i

Jolt

Men's heads pull them
through this suburb like fists,
their trolleys missed and lately collected.
Skin is not equipment
in this shaking off
of targets. Living is all
you digress for:

your heart tuned to the plane's
engine, the slide of air
plateauing at speed,
in what seems certain, blank
and endless – the countenance
of our hostesses.

Primary

Beneath the treacle-blonde
of timber, hard hats yell over perky
commercials, the rumble of obdurate machinery.
The honeycomb of fort-rubble
and battered armour
of croissants, fleeting as a thumb of butter
over popcorn's spongy knuckles.
Crumbs adrift on buzzing water
where Mother Duck tutors
five shivery dablings.
The sting of a yoke-light want
of hatching – a tiny Easter: welcome lights –
Buff-coloured he corrected officiously.

Encarta

Who, over distance,
can outrun

a library? Germans
clambering

over ruins
like *Indiana Jones*.

The years you save
buy nothing –

listlessly
shopping through night,

while others
try on postures.

At the seminar
for jobs

that don't yet exist,
the clip they play

embroidered
in brutal

statistics.
Peace is a word

you could ride
to tenure,

but who would own
this quiet?

Secondary

The aubergine, by the window, glossy
as an eight ball: lavender,
the road, a torn-
open mountain pouring cloud.
Noble erosions from sceptre to cushions,
from mitre to trademark.
A lavish glut of adjectives, dissolving
in a merlot hour – flabby as any
soft landing among
the rubber bells of foxgloves.
The heart as wound or badge, a tattoo
smudged like junk-mail wet.
A fading haze
from clubs like grates where fires have been –
signs hung out as dirty washing.

Proper Opera, a Rom-com

Laws I follow
your lead

in breaking
we kiss

the lights turn
headlines

bright
with recidivism

Reliquary

A mouse makes objects bulge
and quiver, sticky across
possibilities of screen. The bar
clogged with stag nights
so you mouth the words
you would've shouted.
We always wondered at his
aggressive ease. His mistakes

the kind of misspellings
that electrify Maths faculties.
And now you're back on that
family vacation, the same cassette
a soundtrack to dead arms
and crowpecks.

Via Negativa

This is not a knee to get down on:
the insouciant flag a smoker
might fly, the sizzling command
or strong arm of fashion. Not
the vociferous fog of lift-off
nor retrospection's slow erasure,
empty weather for your divination,
not a pipe – not even a picture.
This is not the sticking place,
an en dash or ampersand,
a hot coal cuffed from hand to hand
and dropped into the singeing bed
you walk through for the camera.

Barbarian Studies

Weather in which I might be
elsewhere, lounging
book in hand, *Tim Tams*
(dark, perhaps), tea a given,

instead of the uphill pram push of swaying kids,
singing drunkenly:
what a coachman circa 1840
or his horse felt, probably,

or the wind millennia before,
roughly
when the Vikings (for all their
poetry) at least did their

own rowing –
unlikely as they are to pop up
nowadays
in ads for fathers

with proportional custody;
although they'd do well in this park
where dogs – in loose
and scratchy orbits – nosey about

the margins of
the gated playground
and kids jostle, shove, and swing
like wrecking balls,

like ambassadors
whose sending we regret.
The park is full of aggro dads.
I, poet, am one.

Fixed Terms

Notions of the real
estate pages'
blank canvas or doer upper.

Above the TV's warring
caution,

another doomed family
settee.

Eight Monoscapes

Closing   Headlights scour the civic heart.

Spring   and the great clubfoot of the abbey.

Futures   Two kids on BMXs facing down the rain.

Local   Ned Kelly letterboxes. Suspect crows.

Dark storehouse of the pines. Red Leicester moon.

Late Light   The shed's dull tin. Ripe lemons.

A party   at anchor. Paddock dusty with stars.

Shed Light   Insects hang like burnt-out planets.

Style Guide

weak   government   prose   should   be

a   window   to   see   rhyme   through

the   baby   legs   and   arms   beneath

a   Disney   gallows   doesn't   know

the   words   we   no   longer   kick   with

that roughening of gentle sense that leaves

a   toddler   clutching   spoon   as   dagger

Albums that are Summer

Kids negotiating sun and shade,
gerrymandering sand.

We pick through iTunes
like after Christmas.

The mind empty as a book
of sayings. You'd rather be

on a thatch pontoon
with a bunch of dickheads

according to the ad, and
when the glass breaks,

you admonish
the room, knowing this an audition.

Sprints with Elizabethan Sighs

1.

The clearing weather and sweet
bounce of dial-up
(heard a decade later) have you chasing
a ball and its dog
through valleys you would build from Lego,
if only
they made blocks green.

2.

I'd never rent in a David Lynch film
but others are stuck inside them
or endless meditation
classes in places less
than California.

3.

Every childhood has a dog
bite that grows as the pitches shrink,
like places you remember
from *Monopoly*
too vaguely to pass GO
with the date you talked into the Friday evening quiz.

4.

A cry for help is punctuated the way bestsellers
warn against,
so instead of crowdfunding
a heady rescue, we search for clues
in your parents' wardrobe –
find nothing but functional coats.

5.

The greens and blues
of *California Games* were commensurate
with the lack of skill,
insisted the Professor of Surf Studies,
crying on so
many levels.

6.

Before his conviction
for stealing a roof,
I remember him, whiter than lightning down the left,
gesticulating madly
on the playing fields of youth.

Sprung

I limp the way instinct tells me,

                though I could be

wrong. The paper afternoons

                    fold out beyond

the nests of hope and the petty riot

            of the radio – kindling

for nothing but an angler's quiet.

            There are no rivers

to stamp your name on,

           though rabbits appear

in the grass like little loaves.

           Girls coast by on bikes:

their pretty mouths.

Primary

Sharper than a MiG-jet, your first surfboard
was your last. Waves peel off
the bedroom wall with topical girls
of implausible islands.
All things pass
like Soviet denim: a chill that soaks
the hanging whites.
                           The diving light
of living rooms, in the flash
and wash of temperate news. Amid a rush,
as bright as hail, the servo sets
its welcome. When vendors
take in signs, you hear your mettle
in that cold clank.

Last Post

It goes on
like the joke about daleks and stairs.

Light wriggling off
a star

no longer there.

The shit
we talk through open

summer,
as kindy

shapes
the proper.

Fetch me butchers

paper.

A better answer.

But Soft

Damaged wing
of a song
no louder than the room.
Pax intones my daughter, meaning *fox*.

Quest

I'm searching for a present
more manual
than song: quest
and twist in equal measure.

The truth is that the year
was always ending.
The city cedes ground
to a man who laughs

too loudly – jugglers and hecklers,
the usual thing.
Home is the place to exercise
your subtlety. I shout

my curious thanks
down the bus's bent corridor.

Secondary

Easier to paint
than rhyme, this volatility. A poet-envy
of the art-fluke, or ripeness
cut in segments sucked to the pith.
A plaintive case deflating
on a snack bar counter
where citrus men
swash fizz through lunch
and later repair the voltage of night
in the out-of-sync bounce
of signal and blinker.
You take a little kindling, the light
of a cupped match,
to hazard across deciduous campuses:
the vast, blue continent of theory. Go, softly on.

Notes

The End of Weather: Auslan is a sign-language used by the deaf community in Australia.

Primary: Some researchers contend that students respond better to comments written in colours other than red.

Nth Degree: Mt Sumptuous is a fictitious mountain, 11,483 feet high.

Adventures in Reading: A Gopher is a common brand of motorised mobility scooter.

Immortal Diamond takes its bearings from the Gerard Manley Hopkins poem, *That Nature is a Heraclitean Fire and of the Comfort of the Resurrection*. It has nothing to do with Bob Dylan winning the Nobel Prize for Literature.

Band | Aid: In Australia and the US *Band-Aid*™ has become the generic name for a small adhesive bandage. Band Aid (without the hyphen) was a charity supergroup formed by Bob Geldof and Midge Ure in 1984.

The show *When Animals Attack Celebrities* proved unsuccessful. Although the animals were exotic and the injuries grievous, most of the celebrities were considered too minor. An outtake involving a gang of Barbary macaques and Saxon from *Big Brother* (Season 3) is still popular on *YouTube*.

Room Temperature: The 'proud, bright sail' misremembers Shakespeare's 'proud full sail' from Sonnet 86.

Othello wanted 'ocular proof' such 'that the probation bear no hinge nor loop / To hang a doubt on ...' (Act 3, Scene 3).

Secondary: *Brillo*™ has become the generic name for most scouring pads.

Amstrad® had a sizeable portion of the PC market throughout the '80s. The company was founded by Alan Sugar, who in the '90s served as chairman for Tottenham Hotspur, and brought Jürgen Klinsmann to White Hart Lane. The company's name is a contraction of **Al**an **M**ichael **Sugar Trad**ing.

AI: Skynet is the artificial intelligence defence network that becomes self-aware in the film *The Terminator* and remains so for the film's many sequels.

Logos, as in Brands: The first part of this poem alludes to Robert Frost and Shakira.

Best & Less is an Australian retailer of clothing and household linens. Their wares are competitively priced.

The Thinker is a famous bronze sculpture by Auguste Rodin, though this poem is based on a copy rather than the original.

Founded in the '70s by sociologist Ed (Eggy) Parcels, *Why*'s aim was to be a counterweight to *Who*, selling the glamours of a life of the mind. The magazine ceased publication in 1981.

Beauty Fades, Dumb is Forever, published in 1999, was Judge Judy's second book.

The single-volume encyclopedia the poem's speaker received for his eleventh birthday was fully comprehensive (A–Z).

Diagram & Leaf: Thomas Jefferson was skeptical of stocks, shares and suchlike, referring to them as 'tricks on paper'.

Courtier: Supervised by the police, *Blue Light Discos* began in Australia in the early '80s. All participants were underage, and drinking, drug-taking and sex were only permitted outside the venue.

Weber™ is a brand of barbecue common in Australia.

Moderate: In English law, clergymen could escape trial – and later hanging – at the hands of secular courts by a right known as Benefit of Clergy. The practice was largely reformed under the Tudors but the final vestiges were not done away with until the early 19th Century. The 'neck-verse', usually Psalm 51:1, was read in Latin to prove literacy and so clerical status.

To the only begetter: This poem alludes to Shakespeare's sycophantic dedication in the first edition of *The Sonnets* and literary speculation about this.

Who is the dedicatee? One helpful guess in the *International Journal of Shakespeare Authorship Studies* is that it's the illegitimate son of Queen Elizabeth I, who later became her lover, before a career as a pirate and cryptographer.

Jolt: The phrase 'skin is not equipment' was suggested by a *Skins*™ advert which asserted the opposite. The company has 'a vision of a world in which sport inspires society', and the brand's nothing-to-hide approach has proved popular with those of all ages.

Secondary: *Cadbury*™ trademarked their particular shade of purple in 1995.
The Purple Heart is a high military honour awarded in the name of the US President to those wounded or killed in combat.

Reliquary: 'Aggressive ease' is a phrase Ford Madox Ford used to describe the manner in which Ezra Pound lounged about.
A 'dead arm' is the pain or numbness caused by repeated pummelling of the arm, not necessarily very hard, but for a long duration. 'Crowpecks' are less universal but more brutal and involve making a fist, with one knuckle protruding, and rapping someone repeatedly on the top of the head. They are more effective when their object is approached from behind. *Urban Dictionary* suggests the term originated in Queensland.

Via Negativa: 'The sticking place' is what Macbeth is instructed to screw his courage to by Lady Macbeth in the closing scene of Act I.

Barbarian Studies: The Vikings were alright, as is understood from recent dramatisations.
Gated communities have ancient antecedents and are generally designed to keep barbarians out.

Style Guide: This poem's opening alludes to George Orwell's likening of good prose to a clear window.

Albums that are Summer: This poem refers to a *Corona*™ advert prominent in 2016 and possibly earlier, featuring idealised, but peopled, landscapes and the slogan: 'Where you'd rather be'.

Sprints with Elizabethan Sighs: Elizabethans believed the heart leaks a drop of blood for every sigh.
The David Lynch remark probably doesn't apply to every film, or to every meditation class.

Primary: Yes, 'topical'.

But Soft: The poem's title is taken from the famous line in *Romeo & Juliet*.
Pax is, of course, Latin for knapsack.

Secondary: The final three words of this poem are spoken by Fortinbras in Act 4 of *Hamlet*, when he and the protagonist narrowly miss each other before going their separate ways to the Polak wars and England.

Wakefield Press is an independent publishing and
distribution company based in Adelaide, South Australia.
We love good stories and publish beautiful books.
To see our full range of books, please visit our website at
www.wakefieldpress.com.au
where all titles are available for purchase.
To keep up with our latest releases, news and events,
subscribe to our monthly newsletter.

Find us!

Facebook: www.facebook.com/wakefield.press
Twitter: www.twitter.com/wakefieldpress
Instagram: www.instagram.com/wakefieldpress

9 781743 056646